BRIGHT SIDES OF A DARK JOURNEY

Published by Spines
ISBN: 979-8-89691-478-5

BRIGHT SIDES OF A DARK JOURNEY

A POETIC TESTIMONY

ODREN POLK

CONTENTS

INTRODUCTION

In life, you faced many obstacles, some you have no control over. There are lessons to learn and many things that you go through in life, whether they're good or bad. But are you built to weather the storm, or will you fall victim to the rain? A question I always used to ask myself. I just chose to channel that energy into something more positive, understanding that you can be responsible for your success, or you can be responsible for your downfall. It's all about how bad you really want it. I will never use my hardships in life as an excuse. I never wanted to be a statistic. That's why I chose to put it to some good use.

PART I

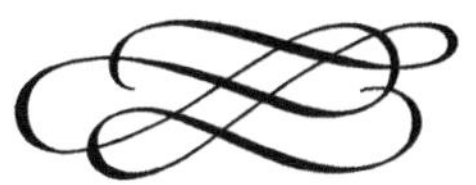

Restricted Area

FRIENEMIES

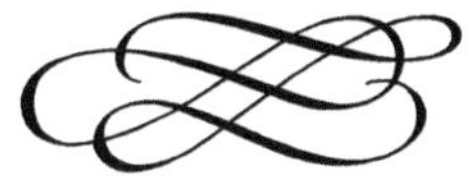

I remember that day I saw you on the show, thinking to myself, having you in my possession will be detrimental to my health. But I decided to take you home and play the cards I was dealt. I carried you everywhere. I must admit, you were a lot of help. You solved a lot of problems all by yourself. I taught you how to write your name on paper and make a mess with fruit. I kept you oiled and cleaned. I tempered you. When you spoke, they listened. Most of all, whenever you gave a warning, everybody paid attention, and all those who stepped out of line understood the business. You were special, well-respected. No one ever tried to check you.

Who ever thought there would be a day when I had to address you? Months went by; I saw no change in you. I thought it was all good. I guess you caught me slipping because I misunderstood. You pulled the wool over my eyes. I didn't know you had other plans. You were headed another route. I guess I got in your way because one strange day, you tried to take my life away. I don't know what was on your mind or what you were thinking. I don't know who got in your head or whatever was stuck in your mind that made you blow. You almost had me too, but God said no. But I forgive you. It was out of your control. You couldn't have possibly known you'd jam—my blood brother, Walther.

THE ROLE MODEL

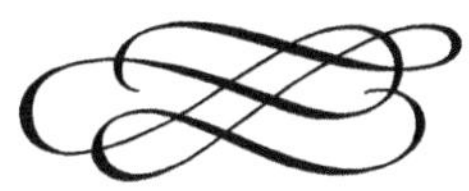

I remember going to school, seeing you on the block, and you running behind the buildings whenever you saw cops. But for some strange reason, you always kept your eyes on me. I didn't know you from anything. I didn't know you from any place. You could've been a kidnapper, a robber, a killer—actually, all of the above if we keep it straight. Why did you choose me out of everybody? Maybe you saw when my mother was on drugs. Maybe you understood why I was surrounded by thugs.

Did you really care about how I looked when I went to school? Did you feel like it was your responsibility? Did you feel like a fool? I wasn't your obligation. We had no ties, but I could see the love in your face every time you looked me in the eyes. I knew you sold drugs of every kind, and I knew you carried guns all the time.

Is there really such a thing as an evil angel? Has to be, my guess—because you're an angel to me but evil to the rest. You were like a father figure I never had. Sold drugs all day, waited for me to get home from school to play dad. They say kids should never talk to strangers, but in some way, we related. I used to laugh when I saw those giant cell phones and pagers.

I remember that conversation we had—if you want nice things, the things I'm asking, you gotta do it. No skipping school, and if you're getting good grades, you gotta prove it. I want to see every report card and the things that you're doing. He saw the look on my face and understood the confusion. So I did everything he asked. I saw my life start to change in a positive way. I went from the average Joe to smiles and hugs from girls I didn't even know.

Heisen Hayes, a lot of problems slowly started to fade. A couple of years went by, and I'm in a stage. Less and less, I would see your face. I looked for you every day until I had to come to terms with the fact that you disappeared without a trace. You changed my life.

THE HOUSE PARTY FROM HELL

It's a Saturday night, me and my manz is chilling. We get a call from a girl. It's a house party tonight, and they want us in the building. No problem—you already know it's baddies in the building. We show up and show out cause that's how we living.

As the night goes on, things get strange. I'm popping fly shit to a baddie while *New Edition's Can You Stand the Rain* plays. A car pulls up with screeching tires. Three men walk in the crib like lions in their den, looking at everybody like fresh food, and the bullshit begins.

One guy lets it be known that he's carrying a hammer—it flashes on his hip. For some reason, there's tears in his eyes, and he's ready to trip. "At first, no! You fucking with another dude? You're about to have my baby? Don't take me for a fool! I'd pop him right now if I thought he was in the room!"

He storms out the door, but at the same time, please, it's smooth—party's over. Everybody's outside, planning their next moves. He's outside, ready to act up, and from the look in his eye, he's ready to send a few packed up. Heavy emotion—I could tell by his posture. He gives the other two a point, like a coach checking the roster.

He walks up, waves a gun. "Let me holler at you!"

Yo, I never hesitated, like, "Yo, what's up?"

"Have you and my baby mother been talking? I need to know what's up!"

I had to let him know—I had no clue what he was talking about. Not to mention, I had never seen him before in my life. He flashed the gun again. He could've popped me, but he didn't.

But the Shorty I was with decided to stand on business, like, "You see him going through this car with me, and you waving around with a gun like you really hard? I see."

I had to explain to him again that it wasn't what it seemed. He was confused. He saw my man run across the street, and it was quickly diffused. He could see the truth in my eyes.

He asked me, "Yo, why did your man run?"

I looked at him with the same confusion and never understood why—betrayal.

THE FATHER FIGURE

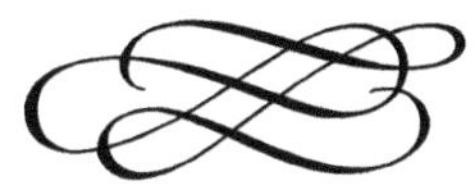

I don't know why I feel this way. I don't know why life really had to be this way. I thought that you would protect me and keep me from harm's way. I looked at you different, felt strong when people spoke of your name. But lil did I know, all of that would change.

You walked around like the world was in your hands. You were confused, cause all in all, you really didn't understand. Times were changing, and you really wasn't built like that. Yeah, you had guns, knives, and bats—but you ain't live like that.

It took one incident for me to see your true self. I despise you. Quietly, out of respect, I kept it to myself.

You are nothing like the people in the street said you was. In fact, you weren't ready to go to war with all those guns, knives, and bats. It was the opposite. Many times, I tried to let it go, but when I looked you in the eyes, I already knew.

That day in the kitchen, I almost left you there forever. I was seconds away from putting you in the earth, burying you in the dirt, people mourning in the church.

But she pushed me out of the way—you lived to breathe another day.

It haunts me in every way. It haunts me every day. She's the reason why I never put a bullet between your face.

I feel betrayed. I'm sorry.

Nobody paid attention, but I watched your every move. You never was genuine. Did nothing out of love. So many nights, I cried, but I would never let a person like you pull the wool over my eyes.

You treated my mother like she didn't belong. Cursed her out, kicked her out, never showed her any love—yet she still respected you. Everybody ignored it. I saw way through it.

Did nothing but disrespect her instead of help her through it. Every time I looked at you, I saw blood in my eyes. I was numb to the lies. And every time you tried to beat me, I never cried or showed emotion. I could never give you that satisfaction, cause deep down in my heart, I really wanted all the action.

.25 automatic under my pillow—I could've killed you with ease. But that wouldn't have been fair, cause I really wanted you to bleed.

I feel betrayed. I'm sorry.

PART II

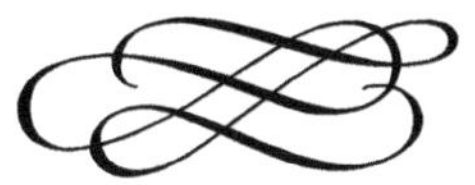

SHE UNDERSTOOD

I remember coming home from school, walking in the door, seeing nothing in the house—no pictures on the wall, no TVs, no couch. So much anger and confusion. My body was shaking. I wanted to lose it, but the pain in my soul would not let me do it. So this is what life is about. Mixed the heroin with the crack cocaine, you sell everything that's in the house—even your spouse. It's not just a habit. Some addicts are really savage.

I walk upstairs into the room—nothing but clothes scattered on the floor. She even sold the bedframe and the mattress. I'm talking here today, gone in seconds like a hat trick. Late at night, I hear music blasting—strangers in the house. Wasn't allowed to go downstairs 'cause strangers in the house. A foul smoke clogged my lungs because of the **ing** strangers in the house. They were dirty, nasty. They moved slow and looked half-dead—like zombies in my house.

I had a shorty with me. She understood about the house. She shed tears.

"Is this really ya house?"

"Nah, we're going to my house."

She understood!!!!

FALSE LIFE

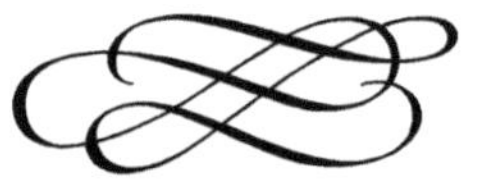

Growing up, I thought every kid should have two parents, a house with a picket fence. Boy, was that a reach, and I couldn't get an inch. I stayed with the blues without the prints, all because of drought—fishbowls without the tints.

Could never figure out why the hand-me-downs weren't handy. So much aggression tucked inside—they could never understand me. And every time they judged, I gained another piece of sanity. And every disappointment moved me further from my family.

I'm just venting. The therapy didn't help. Wishing I could've given Cuz a kidney to fix his health. I'm on my knees making du'a, praying for wealth. If you've been where I've been, then you know where I'm going.

Happy
Boardwal

WHAT HUNGER DOES

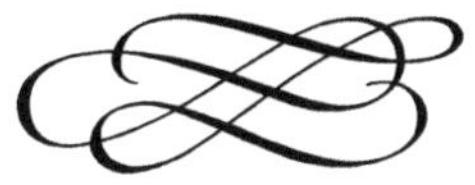

I wake up full of pain and resentment. Stomach growling —haven't eaten since the day before. I don't get it. I ask God why He left me with a bad prison sentence.

Ten years old, thinking about going to war in the trenches, not caring about the ending—because at this point in time, it's survival of the fittest. But I'm built, though, and for some strange reason, I'm willing to take it as far as it may go.

I try to ignore it, but the hunger just won't let go. My mind just won't say no. I swear, I'd risk it all for a slice of bread and an egg roll. The desperation is relentless. And every time I sleep it off, I get more tempted.

Why would a baby this young be thinking this senseless? You tell me.

THE GOOD BAD DECISION

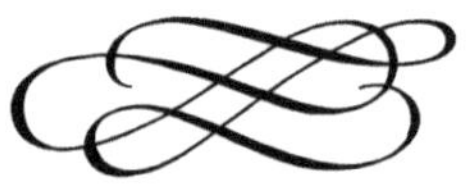

I often wonder how my life would have been had you still on 10, but instead, you left me in the jungle, hiding in the rubble, knowing every place I looked and everywhere I turned was trouble. They say hurt people hurt people. It's to prove in fact, but how could you function knowing I couldn't function—not knowing where I was until I understood where I was was all because of you. You just disappeared. Never took the time to check, not knowing if I was good or bad, happier or sad, hungry or full. So much anger tucked inside of me, so much resentment in my face—I could never hide it in me. Did you think or even know what you were doing? I understand you couldn't possibly understand the life you were ruining. It wasn't the fact of not seeing; it's the fact that I understood you were being haunted by your demons. You weren't being treated fairly—an outcast even. And every time you tried to show your face, they forced you into leaving. Because they would never allow you to stop the money they were receiving. I know it's a long story, too hurtful to tell, but you have to understand my side, even though I know you meant well.

WATER THAT IS THICKER THAN BLOOD

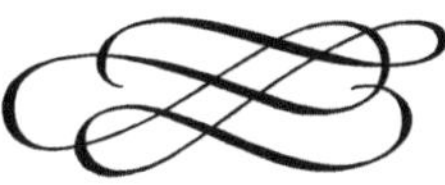

My brother always had my back. I remember a lot of people used to talk crazy, but you were never having that. I remember a lot of girls used to try to front—you weren't going for that. Two different mentalities, but the same love for each other. You came fresh off the block. I came fresh out the gutter. I could talk to you about anything, come to you about anything. Nobody wanted to smoke at all, 'cause he was with all and everything. I wrote this about you because, at times, I miss you. Once, I thought we were enemies. I thought we were opposites —until that one day in school when we related on the same topic. Do you remember that talk we had about life? Shit felt different. It was comforting. It was right. A brother that I never knew was right in front of me. Yeah, we cracked jokes on each other and the occasional diss, but I noticed that you never let dudes play with me. When I was around you, I was able to exist. I got so much love for you, bro. I had to write it down. It's too much that I could say—it's too much to remember. You've always been in the streets, popping your shit—that's no lie. You've always walked it how you talked. You were built to survive. I knew that from the beginning; I've been witnessed. You made me feel like I could do the same— that's why I always still doing business. A real one.

PART III

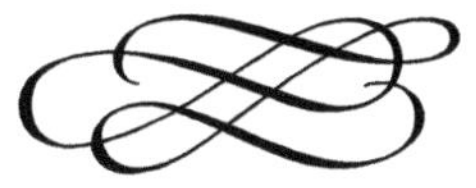

THE DEVIL'S CANDY

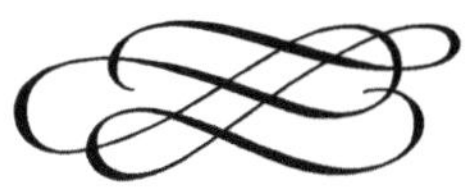

It took a while—wow—but I understand now how you couldn't put the drugs down. No guidance, left alone, crying, stuck in the wild, surrounded by lions. No turning back—you felt like dying, headed to hell, no direction, untaught lessons, invisible blessings. Nothing to lose, so you max out, demons watching your every move. Every sign of redemption, they smothered you. It was your soul they needed to control you. All you needed was someone to hold. Instead, they ridiculed and scolded you. Nowhere to go but further down, in and out different cars, in and out of town—a lost soul down an even darker road.

But what do you do when all your resources are finished, when all your finances are done, and your high is at the end? The pain starts again, and the walls start closing in. And you're back on your mission—lies and deceit never cease to cease. You can never get any peace because the thing that you acquire most won't allow you to sleep, allow you to function, allow you to eat. Because you're no longer in control of that body—it belongs to the demuns.

You try to seek help, but all the doors are locked. You try to call for support, but the calls are blocked. Rips on all your clothes, dirt and filth over your socks. Your hair damaged, hardly touched. Your body, mingled and misused, partly bruised. Bury yourself, or crawl into the light—

Which one would you choose?

Or is it even a choice?

Dark.

A
HOOD CONFESSION (1)

Hi, can I talk to you for a minute? Have you ever seen a ghetto? Have you ever walked through the trenches? I'm talking big brick buildings surrounded by tall fences. I don't think you have, and I'm glad. So listen—there's nothing near but drugs, guns, pussy for sale, and nice cars. Also filled with famous people, drug dealers, and people who rob.

You gotta be built to survive in the jungle, 'cause one wrong move could be your last. A hustle could be your last breath. Could be your death. But if I were you, I'd walk along the sidewalks. Stay on the steps, because jumping off the porch—you better know what you're doing, because the streets know what the streets know. Move wisely, 'cause that life is very contagious. Just ask Ronald Isley.

I've seen many come, many go, many shot—and I'm not even scratching the surface of the plot. You can be in the wrong place for the right reason, and it won't explain a lot. Even the innocent get tested. It's treacherous. There were times I had to pick up guns just to walk through sections. I know it's a lot. We've got a lot more to go, so please pay attention.

A
HOOD CONFESSION (2

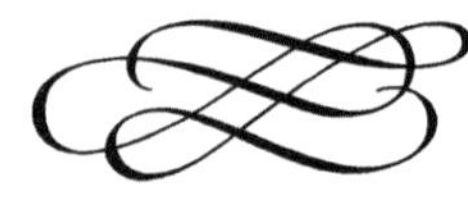

They say we all get the same 24 hours. Well, I'm gonna have to disagree. I can remember coming outside at 9 AM and a dude from my neighborhood getting shot by three. I see that. The saying is "believe none of what you hear and only half of what you see." Life can be very difficult depending on your geography and environment. And I can promise you this—seeing violence every day can be very tiring.

It's OK to read books and study your arts. Growing up in the 90s, you had to be Mr. Miyagi—which is street smarts. I gotta be honest—life was hard for me, but I knew if I had to, I could get down and dirty, filthy. I never liked that kind of energy. And I always had a plan, even though the odds were against me. And I always told myself, for a statistic, I would never be highly aggressive but yet peaceful.

I told myself I would never end up like my people, and no matter what it took—all these hardships—I would see them through. I grew up with dudes that robbed, stole, chilled, kidnapped, and hustled. And the funny part is—they were doing all of that, and in my eyes, it looked like they were still struggling.

You saw a group of dudes make so much money that they stress it, and they gotta walk around with an AK and a Uzi to protect it. Oh no, well, I have. We're not the same. You outta place—I really come from that. Don't ever make that mistake.

PTSD

Where were you? I looked everywhere for years. I tried to track you down. But you just left me in the box with no one to claim, as if I was the lost and found. I never really understood what went wrong, and yet still, I could never get any honest answers at all. It made my blood boil—mass mental confusion. I would walk past—memories of your face would pop up. That's an illusion. It wasn't you. It wasn't your presence. I felt nothing. But I could never get over the fact of needing you for something. Nothing came easy. In fact, a big chaotic mess. I guess you forgot that you left something behind—the same as Rick. I promised to trust you. You lost it.

When I look outside my window, I see bricks, concrete, and guns. Addicts pace the avenue, cups in the hands of bums. But I felt the same as they did because all we ate were crumbs, and the smell of toxic smoke consumes my lungs. From the outside, it feels like I'm stuck in hell with no hope. I'm drowning in sharky waters, hoping someone throws me a rope. At night,

I can hear the screech of mice in the kitchen. I can't get comfortable from the feeling of roaches—every so often touching my skin—now I'm itching. I live in hell. Outside, nothing but fire and demons. As I walk the streets, I can feel them all around, on my neck, breathing. But it's normal, not just for me but for many others. We're all going through the same thing. We all suffer, and hard situations turn your best friend into your brother— because we need each other.